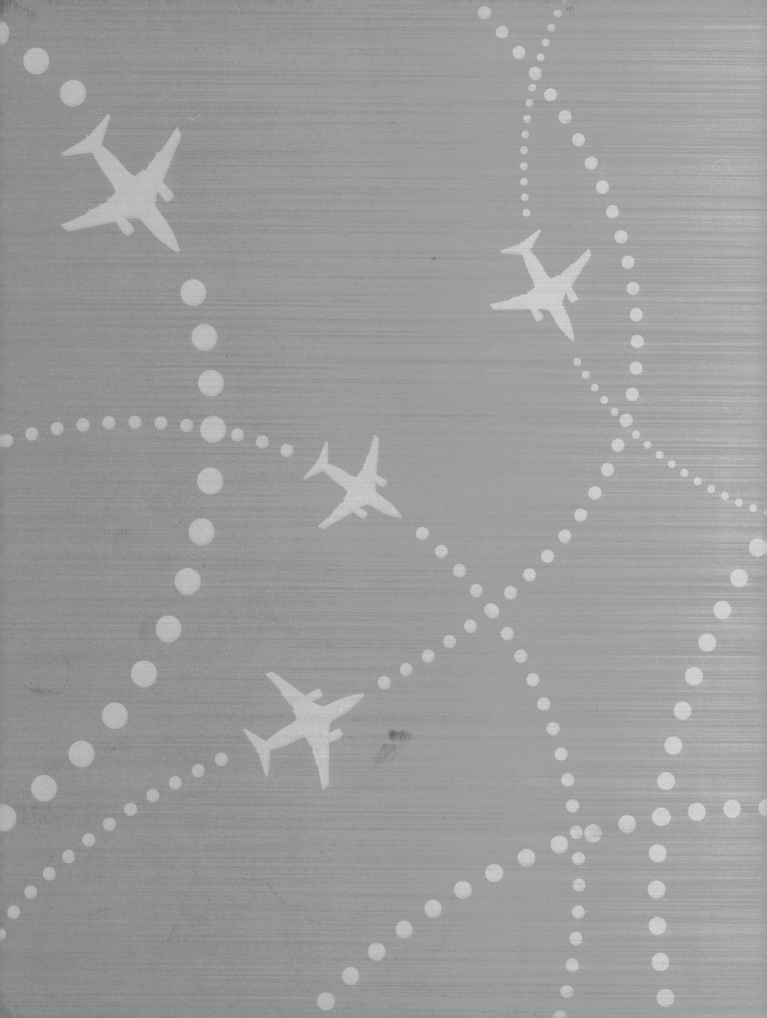

Planes and Helicopters

Clive Gifford

WAYLAND

First published in 2012 by Wayland

Copyright © Wayland 2012

Wayland
338 Euston Road
London NW1 3BH

Wayland Australia
Level 17/207 Kent Street
Sydney, NSW 2000

Editor: Nicola Edwards
Designer: Elaine Wilkinson
Picture Researcher: Clive Gifford

British Library Cataloguing in Publication
Data

Gifford, Clive.
    Planes and Helicopters. --
(Machines at work)
    1. Airplanes--Juvenile literature.
    2. Helicopters--Juvenile literature.
    I. Title II. Series
    629.1'3334-dc23

ISBN: 978 0 7502 6886 8

Printed in China

Wayland is a division of Hachette Children's
Books, an Hachette UK company

www.hachette.co.uk

To find out about the author, visit his website:
www.clivegifford.co.uk

Picture acknowledgements:
The author and publisher would like to thank
the following agencies and people for allowing
these pictures to be reproduced:
Cover (main) ssuaphotos / Shutterstock.
com, (inset) Balazs Toth / Shutterstock.
com; title page Steve Mann / Shutterstock.
com, p3 Sascha Hahn / Shutterstock.com;
p4 (t) Christopher Parypa / Shutterstock.
com, (b) Robert Crum / Shutterstock.
com; p5 Natali Glado / Shutterstock.com;
p6 Pablo Scapinachis / Shutterstock.com;
p7 (t) Robert Rozbora / Shutterstock.com,
(b) karamysh / Shutterstock.com; p8 Sascha
Hahn / Shutterstock.com; p9 (t) Eugene
Berman / Shutterstock.com, (b) Khafizov
Ivan Harisovich / Shutterstock.com; p10 (l)
David Acosta Allely / Shutterstock.com, (r)
courtesy of AgustaWestland; p11 jakelv7500
/ Shutterstock.com; p12 Carlos E. Santa
Maria / Shutterstock.com; p13 (t) iStock
© Simon Parker, (b) Michael G Smith /
Shutterstock.com; p14 (l) Maurizio Milanesio
/ Shutterstock.com, (r) David Fowler /
Shutterstock.com; p15 dvande / Shutterstock.
com; p16 Steve Mann / Shutterstock.
com; p17 (t) Louise Cukrov / Shutterstock.
com, (b) R McIntyre / Shutterstock.com;
p18 Andrej Poi / Shutterstock.com; p19 (t)
Maria Hetting / Shutterstock.com, (b) Steve
Mann / Shutterstock.com; p20 iStock © Eric
Gevaert; p21 (t) Remzi / Shutterstock.com
(b) Losevsky Pavel / Shutterstock.com; p23
Christopher Parypa / Shutterstock.com; p24
Balazs Toth / Shutterstock.com

Contents

Flying machines at work

Planes and helicopters are flying machines. They leave the ground and fly high through the air carrying people and cargo from place to place.

A plane takes off from an airport with more than 100 passengers on board.

Jet engines

ZOOM IN

This part of a plane is called the cockpit. It's here that the pilot sits and operates the controls of the plane.

Planes and helicopters are used for many different jobs, from carrying airmail packages and taking aerial photographs to spraying crops in farm fields and rescuing climbers trapped on mountainsides.

Tail

Wings help lift the aircraft off the ground and keep it in the air

FAST FACT
Around 2,750 million passengers flew on airliners in 2011.

Rotor blades spin lifting helicopter into air

Cockpit where pilot sits

A small helicopter takes off from the ground. Its passengers will get a bird's-eye view of the land below.

Tail

Landing skids

Planes and helicopters are very heavy machines. They need to create a force called lift to help them rise into the air when they take off. A plane's wings and a helicopter's rotor blades are the parts that create lift.

A large airliner takes off. Its four engines provide the thrust to move it forward while its large wings generate plenty of lift.

A wing is curved on top and flatter along the bottom. This is called an aerofoil shape. When a wing moves forward, air flows over and under it at different speeds. This helps create lift. A helicopter rotor blade has an aerofoil shape, just like a plane wing.

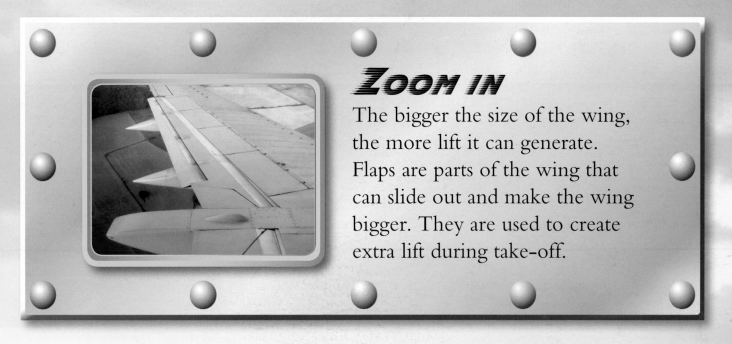

ZOOM IN

The bigger the size of the wing, the more lift it can generate. Flaps are parts of the wing that can slide out and make the wing bigger. They are used to create extra lift during take-off.

A small helicopter takes off from a patch of grass at an airfield. As the rotor blades swoop through the air, they generate lift.

Moving forward

Engines provide the power to move planes forward through the air. Some planes can travel very long distances and reach really high speeds, far faster than other types of transport.

This military plane is powered by two jet engines.

FAST FACT

The SR71 Blackbird is the fastest ever jet plane. It can reach speeds of over 3,000km/h – three times the speed of a regular jet airliner.

Hot gases leave the engines at the rear

Cockpit holds the pilot and co-pilot

Jet engines are used to power many large airliners and fast military planes. Other planes use propellers. These are long, thin blades which are turned by an engine and pull the plane through the air.

This C130 Hercules plane has four engines, each spinning a propeller around. This plane is used by the US Coastguard to patrol coastlines, carry cargo and perform rescue operations.

ZOOM IN

Jet engines suck in air and mix it with fuel before setting the mixture alight. The burning mixture creates gases which expand out of the back of the engine, pushing the plane forward.

How do helicopters fly?

Helicopters are amazing flying machines which can take off straight upwards. Instead of fixed wings, a helicopter has long, thin moving blades called rotors.

Rotor blades spin

Cockpit where the pilot sits

Engine underneath this panel turns the rotor blades round at high speed

The pilot spins the rotor blades faster to make the helicopter climb upwards or slower so that it travels downwards.

The pilot of this helicopter has tilted its rotors forward so that they push some air backwards. This thrusts the helicopter forwards.

Zoom in

At the back of a helicopter, a small set of rotors spins in the tail. These tail rotors control the movement of the helicopter to the right and the left.

The helicopter's engine spins the rotor blades quickly. As they slice through the air, they generate enough lift to raise the helicopter up.

Tail rotor

I-PTFT

These long flat bars are called skids

In the cockpit

Pilots sit and control planes and helicopters from the cockpit. There are lots of controls to use and screens and dials to check. They also have a radio system to communicate with airports and other aircraft.

Navigation display   Engine indicators   Engine throttles

Control column

The flight deck of an airliner is packed with controls and instruments. These give the pilot information about the plane and show how all of its parts are performing.

In large planes, such as a passenger airliner, a co-pilot sits alongside the pilot in the cockpit. The co-pilot helps with many tasks and can take over from the pilot to fly the plane at times.

ZOOM IN

This cockpit instrument shows the pilot whether the plane is flying level and whether it is climbing (flying upwards) or descending (flying downwards).

A plane flies past an airport's air traffic control tower. Controllers inside the tower organise the order in which planes take off and land at an airport. They use radios to talk to pilots.

Steering through the sky

Pilots steer planes or helicopters from the cockpit using a control column or joystick. When they are flying from place to place they use the cockpit instruments to find their way.

This helicopter pilot flies his plane using a control stick, a little like a computer game joystick.

Panels on the wings and tail of a plane can be moved up or down
or from side to side. These panels are called control surfaces.
They help to direct the movement of the air around the plane
and keep the plane moving in one direction.

Tail

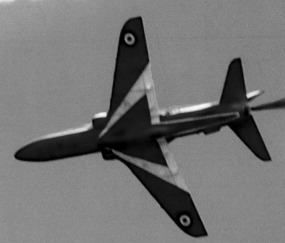

Ailerons in the wing can tilt up or
down to help the plane turn

Planes fly in an aerobatic display to entertain a
crowd. The pilots can make their aircraft spin
round, dive down sharply towards the ground
or fly in a loop, tracing a large circle in the sky.

ZOOM IN

The hinged rear part of the tail is
called the rudder. It helps the plane
steer right or left. Elevators on the
tailplane are hinged flaps which
help the plane fly up or down.

Landing

Most planes land on a runway using their landing gear. These are sets of wheels that are raised up into the body of the plane during the flight but are lowered for landing.

FAST FACT

A Boeing 777 airliner lands at a speed of 245-285 km/h and needs around 1,700m of runway to come to a stop safely.

This plane's landing gear has 10 wheels covered in rubber tyres. The wheels have to support the whole weight of the airliner when it is on the ground.

ZOOM IN

To land a helicopter, the pilot slows the speed of the rotor blades. This creates less lifting force and allows the helicopter to travel gently downwards.

Not all planes land on wheels. Flying boats take-off and land on water. They have large curved bodies that float on water. In snowy locations, planes and helicopters may be fitted with skis or skids to land on instead of wheels.

This Twin Otter seaplane lands in the Indian Ocean. Instead of wheels, the plane uses large floats that allow it to sit on top of the water when it lands.

Helicopters at work

Helicopters can take off straight upwards, fly forwards and even hover in mid-air. This makes them very useful for lots of different jobs. For example, helicopters can reach and rescue injured climbers trapped on a mountainside.

This helicopter hovers in mid-air as a crew member travels down on a strong cable to rescue a person trapped in the sea. The two people will then be winched up back into the helicopter.

Helicopters are good at flying to hard-to-reach places. As they can take off straight upwards, they do not need a long runway. Instead they can fly to and from a helipad or a small area of ground. Helipads can be found on ships and on the roofs of tall city buildings.

ZOOM IN

This helipad is on an oil rig in the middle of the sea. Helicopters can ferry oil rig workers and supplies to and from the rig.

This Chinook helicopter has two pairs of rotor blades. It can lift heavy loads like this jeep and trailer and fly them to another location.

Carrying passengers

Some planes carry enormous loads through the air. Airliners fly hundreds of passengers and their luggage between airports all over the world. A plane's hold is where passengers' luggage and other cargo such as airmail parcels are stored.

Hold

An airliner is unloaded at an airport. The plane needs to be cleaned, refuelled and then loaded with new passengers and their luggage before it makes another flight.

FAST FACT

The biggest airliner of all is the Airbus A380. It can carry up to 853 passengers.

ZOOM IN

Inside the airliner, seats are placed in rows separated by walkways called aisles. Passengers can store small bags, called hand luggage, in cupboards called overhead lockers.

A row of airliners, each parked at a separate gate at an airport. The tunnels are passenger walkways that connect the airliners to the airport buildings.

Quiz

How much have you found out about planes and helicopters at work? Try this quick quiz!

1. What name is given to the person who controls and flies a plane or helicopter?
a) An air traffic controller
b) A pilot
c) An engineer

2. Which part of a plane helps it to fly higher or lower?
a) elevators
b) rudder
c) artificial horizon

3. What type of plane lands on water using its curved, floating body?
a) ski plane
b) seaplane
c) flying boat

4. What does a helicopter have in place of fixed wings?
a) rotor blades
b) flaps
c) propellers

5. What force do plane wings generate when the plane moves forward?
a) friction
b) thrust
c) lift

6. What is the world's biggest airliner?
a) Boeing 747
b) Airbus A380
c) Boeing 777

7. What part of a helicopter helps it steer to the left or right?
a) tail rotor
b) skids
c) main rotor

8. Where is luggage and cargo part stored in a plane?
a) the cockpit
b) the wings
c) the hold

Answers: 1.b, 2.a, 3.c, 4.a, 5.c, 6.b, 7.a, 8.c

Glossary

aerobatic display
spectacular stunts,
such as loops and rolls
usually performed by special planes to
thrill spectators

ailerons   movable edges of the wings that can tilt up or down to help a plane turn

airliner   a large aircraft which carries many passengers and their luggage

cockpit   the part of the plane which contains the plane's controls and where the pilot sits

co-pilot   a trained pilot who sits alongside or behind the pilot and can take over from him or her

elevators   flaps on the tailplane which can move to help the plane climb higher into the air or dive down to fly lower

flight deck   the control panel in the cockpit of an aircraft

helipad   a small area, usually marked with the letter H, from which helicopters take off and land

hold   the part of a plane where luggage and cargo is stored

landing gear   the parts of a plane that contact with the ground or water when it lands

lift   an upwards force generated by a plane's wings or a helicopter's rotor blades

luggage   the suitcases, backpacks and other passenger bags carried on planes

propeller   turning blade that helps thrust a plane forward through the air

rotor   a long thin 'wing' spun by a helicopter's engine to create lift

rudder   a movable flap in a plane's tail that helps it steer

runway   a strip of level ground, usually covered in a smooth surface, from which planes take off and land

take off   the point at which a plane leaves the ground and starts flying through the air

Further Information

Books

On The Go: Planes – David and Penny Glover, Wayland, 2009
Modern Military Aircraft – Daniel Gilpin, Wayland, 2012
Machines On The Move: Helicopters – Andrew Langley, Franklin Watts, 2011

Websites

http://www.avkids.com/
A great website with games and features on planes and even a free downloadable book about business jets.

http://www.ueet.nasa.gov/StudentSite/
Learn about the history of flight, parts of a plane and how jet engines work as this website.

http://rotored.arc.nasa.gov/
Read the story of Robin Whirlybird and see galleries of all sorts of helicopters from the past and present.

Places to Visit

Imperial War Museum, Duxford, Cambridgeshire, CB22 4QR
http://www.iwm.org.uk/visits/iwm-duxford
This huge museum includes a Concorde supersonic airliner among its many planes.

The Helicopter Museum, Locking Moor Road, Weston-super-Mare, Somerset, BS24 8PP
http://helicoptermuseum.co.uk/index.htm
The world's largest collection of helicopters with over 80 on display.

Index

MACHINES AT WORK

Contents of all the titles in the series:

WAYLAND